GREAT RIVERS

The
GANGES

Michael Pollard

BENCHMARK BOOKS

MARSHALL CAVENDISH
NEW YORK

Benchmark Books
Marshall Cavendish Corporation
99 White Plains Road
Tarrytown, New York 10591

American edition © Marshall Cavendish Corporation 1998

First published in 1997 by Evans Brothers Limited
© Evans Brothers Limited 1997

Library of Congress Cataloging-in-Publication Data
Pollard, Michael, date.
    The Ganges / Michael Pollard.
        p. cm. — (Great rivers)
    Includes bibliographical references and index.
    Summary: Traces the course of this famous river in India and describes its physical features, history, and importance.
    ISBN 0-7614-0504-6 (lib. bdg.)
    1. Ganges River (India and Bangladesh)—Juvenile literature. 2. Ganges River Valley (India and Bangladesh)—Juvenile literature. [1. Ganges River. (India and Bangladesh)] I. Title. II. Series: Pollard, Michael, date. Great rivers.
DS485.G25065 1998
954'.1—dc21   97-17017
                                                    CIP
                                                    AC

Printed in Hong Kong

ACKNOWLEDGEMENTS

For permission to reproduce copyright material, the author and publishers gratefully acknowledge the following:

Cover (main image) David Sutherland/Tony Stone Images (left) Jagdeep Rajput/Planet Earth Pictures (right) Mark Hakansson/Panos Pictures Title page Mark Edwards/Still Pictures
page 8 (left) David Cumming (right) Antoinette Jongern/Colorific **page 9** Earth Satellite Corporation/Science Photo Library **page 10** (top) David Beatty/Robert Harding Picture Library (bottom) Graham Buchan/Life File **page 11** Paul Harrison/Still Pictures **page 12** Travel Ink/Ronald Badkin page 13 Ann and Bury Peerless **page 14** (top) Dave Brinicombe/Hutchison Library (bottom) Christine Osborne Pictures **page 15** (top) Ann and Bury Peerless (bottom) Paul Smith/Panos Pictures **page 16** Penny Tweedie/Panos Pictures **page 17** Penny Tweedie/Panos Pictures **page 18** (top) Trip/H Rogers (bottom) Ann and Bury Peerless **page 19** Ann and Bury Peerless **page 20** (top) Dave Brinicombe/Hutchison Library (bottom) David Cumming **page 21** Dave Brinicombe/Hutchison Library **page 22** David Cumming **page 23** David Cumming **page 24** Ann and Bury Peerless **page 25** David Cumming **page 26** A F Kersting **page 27** (top) Liba Taylor/Panos Pictures (bottom) Paul Harris/Tony Stone Images **page 28** David Sutherland/Tony Stone Images **page 29** (top) Hutchison Library (bottom) Hutchison Library **page 30** Nancy Durrell McKenna/Panos Pictures **page 31** (left) Gil Moti/Still Pictures (right) Paul Harris/Tony Stone Images **page 32** Barbara Klass/Panos Pictures (inset) Julio Etchart/Reportage/Still Pictures **page 33** Nancy Durrell McKenna/Hutchison Library (bottom) John Paul Kay/Still Pictures **page 34** (left) B. Klass/Panos Pictures (right) Trygve Bylstad/Panos Pictures **page 35** (top) Gil Moti/Still Pictures (bottom) Paul Harrison/Still Pictures **page 36** Hartmut Schwarzbach/Still Pictures **page 37** Robert Harding Picture Library **page 38** (top) Cobis-Bettmann (bottom) Roland Seitre/Still Pictures **page 39** Jagdeep Rajput/Planet Earth Pictures **page 40** Hutchison Library **page 41** (top and bottom) David Cumming **page 42** (top) Trygve Bolstad/Panos (bottom) Paul Smith/Panos Pictures **page 43** Paul Smith/Panos Pictures

CONTENTS

THE HOLY GANGES 8
THE MAKING OF THE GANGES 10
THE EMPIRE-BUILDERS 12
BELIEFS AND BELIEVERS 14
INDIA AND BANGLADESH 16
TALES OF THE GANGES 18
OUT OF THE MOUNTAINS 20
THE GANGES PLAIN 22
VILLAGES ON THE PLAIN 24
CITIES OF THE PLAIN 26
VARANASI 28
CALCUTTA 30
THE GANGES DELTA 32
PEOPLE OF THE DELTA 34
VISITING THE GANGES 36
THE WILDLIFE OF THE GANGES 38
THE POLLUTED GANGES 40
THE FUTURE 42
GLOSSARY 44
INDEX 45

THE HOLY GANGES

THE GANGES IS INDIA'S LONGEST RIVER. IT FLOWS EASTWARDS ACROSS NORTHERN INDIA FROM THE WESTERN HIMALAYAS TO THE BAY OF BENGAL.

◄ *For Bangladesh, on the Ganges delta, the river is a vital source of food. Here, fishermen prepare their boats for the day's work netting their catch in the delta's waters.*

THE HIMALAYAS separate the Indian subcontinent, which consists of India, Pakistan and Bangladesh, from the rest of Asia. It is the world's highest mountain range, towering to over 2625 feet (800 meters), and includes the world's eight highest mountains. Over 1393 feet (425 meters) up, near the western end of the Himalayas, is the Gangotri glacier. This vast sheet of ice is 15 miles (24 kilometers) long and 5 miles (8 kilometers) wide. Spring and summer meltwater pours from the Gangotri glacier into the Bhagirathi. This is the longest of many mountain streams that join to form the Ganges.

FOOD FOR MILLIONS

The Ganges, or "Ganga" as Indians call it, flows parallel to the Himalayas as it crosses northern India, but flows between 155 and 249 miles (250 and 400 kilometers) south of the mountain range. From the mountains its tributaries bring down water filled with sediment – fragments of rock ground down into mud and sand – creating a wide, fertile plain that provides food for about 300 million people. For the last 311 miles (500

▲ *At Hardwar, on the upper Ganges, Hindus bathe in the Ganges at the festival of Kumbh Mela, India's largest Hindu gathering. It is held every 12 years. The next Kumbh Mela will be in 1998.*

kilometers) of its course, the river flows through Bangladesh. To the Bangladeshi people the river is known as the "Padma." It crosses a delta made up of sediment carried downstream over thousands of years. The Ganges shares the delta with another major river, the Brahmaputra, which flows in from the north, as well as some smaller rivers. It finally reaches the Indian Ocean in the Bay of Bengal, 1554 miles (2500 kilometers) from its source. On its way, it has collected rainwater from an area of 432,432 square miles (1,120,000 square kilometers), which is about twice the size of France.

For six months each year, from May to October, heavy rain sweeps across the Ganges delta and plain. It is brought by winds from

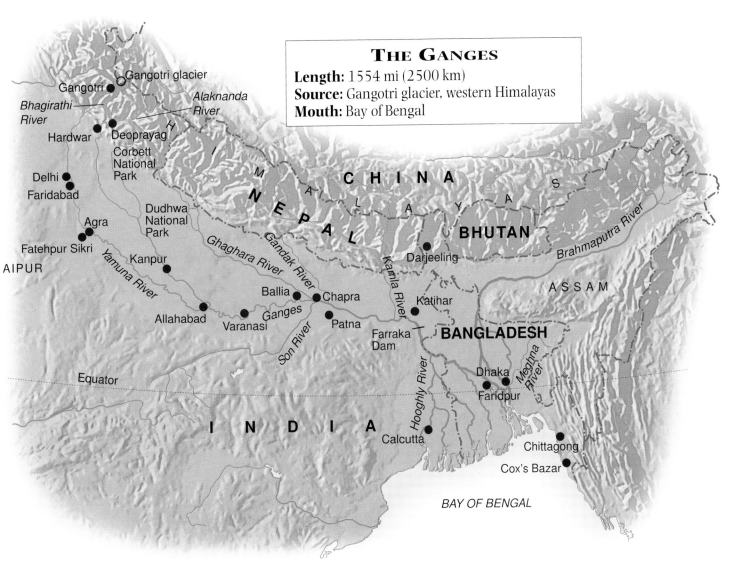

THE GANGES

Length: 1554 mi (2500 km)
Source: Gangotri glacier, western Himalayas
Mouth: Bay of Bengal

the Indian Ocean. This is known as the summer monsoon. The monsoon rain eventually drains into the Ganges and its tributaries.

WORSHIPING THE RIVER

More than eight out of ten Indians are followers of the Hindu religion, and for them the Ganges has a special importance. They believe it is a holy river, the home on Earth of the goddess Ganga. As part of their worship, Hindus drink the water of the Ganges, bathe in it, and many arrange for their ashes to be scattered on the river when they die. There are shrines at many places on the river banks. Hindu pilgrims come to worship at these shrines and they collect Ganges water to take home for their families. For Hindus, the Ganges is much more than a river that waters their crops. It is the center of their lives.

◀ *A false-color satellite image of the Ganges delta, taken in February in the middle of the dry season. The Ganges is the river flowing in from the left. Joining it from the top of the picture is the Brahmaputra. The red areas are crops that are almost ready for harvest. The pale blue areas dotted with red are paddy-fields that are ready for rice-planting. The gray-green areas toward the bottom are swampland.*

THE MAKING OF THE GANGES

About 100 million years ago, great changes were taking place on the Earth's surface. The outer layer, or crust, had split into separate pieces and was floating on a sea of molten rock below.

One of the separate pieces was the Indian sub-continent. Over millions of years, it split away from southern Africa and moved steadily northeast, until it collided with Asia. The colliding edges folded upwards to form the Himalayas. This process also took millions of years, and is still going on. The sudden movement of pieces of the Earth's crust can cause earthquakes. This happened in 1991 at the remote town of Uttarkashi in the upper Ganges valley. Over 1000 people were killed, but the death toll would have been far higher if the area had been more heavily populated.

HIMALAYAN GLACIERS

The mountain peaks of the Himalayas are covered with snow and ice throughout the year. The snowfields and glaciers are the remains of a vast ice-sheet that covered the

▶ *The Bhagirathi, one of the rivers that joins others to form the Ganges. The sides of the valley have been terraced to provide narrow strips of land for farming. Terracing helps to retain soil on the hillsides and prevent it from being washed into the river below.*

◀ *A mountain peak in the Himalayas near the source of the Ganges. Its sharp edges and the deep valley below were carved by glaciers thousands of years ago.*

▶ *Jute, used to make canvas and burlap, is one of the crops of the Ganges delta. After it is harvested, it is dried in the sun before being sent to market. There are few roads on the delta, and rivers are the main highways.*

MAIN TRIBUTARIES OF THE GANGES		
Yamuna: 854 mi (1375 km) joins at Allahabad		
Ghaghara: 603 mi (970 km) joins near Ballia		
Gandak: 590 mi (950 km) joins near Patna		
Son: 487 mi (784 km) joins near Chapra		
Kamla: 435 mi (700 km) joins near Katihar		

Himalayas up to about 18,000 years ago. When this sheet began to thaw, the meltwater carved out hundreds of deep gullies in the southern slopes of the mountains. These gullies became the streams that flow down to form the Ganges and its Himalayan tributaries.

THE GANGES PLAIN

South of the Himalayas, a deep hollow was created by the force of the collision between the Indian and Asian sections of the Earth's crust. This hollow is now the great Ganges plain. The rocks lying beneath the plain have been covered with sediment, which has created rich, fertile soil. The plain is almost flat, so the Ganges flows slowly across it except in the rainy season when the plain is flooded.

THE WORLD'S LARGEST DELTA

As it flows on, the Ganges receives more water from its tributaries. They are carrying sediment from the Himalayas to the north and the lower Vindhya mountains to the south. After crossing the border between India and Bangladesh, it is joined from the north by another of southern Asia's major rivers, the Brahmaputra. Over 1802 miles (2900 kilometers) long, the Brahmaputra flows out of the eastern Himalayas. It is filled with sediment from the mountains. As the slow-flowing waters of the Ganges and the Brahmaputra meet, they are joined by a third river, the Meghna. The Meghna drains the northern slopes of the Assam plateau. The meeting of these three rivers has created the world's largest delta, which has built up over thousands of years. At the sea's edge, the sand and mud form an area of muddy islands covered with mangroves that twist and mat together to make dense thickets. This area is known as the "Sundarbans." The tides of the Bay of Bengal rise and fall among these islands, where the Ganges finally meets the sea.

THE EMPIRE-BUILDERS

FOR THOUSANDS OF YEARS, THE HISTORY OF THE GANGES VALLEY WAS ONE OF RAIDS AND INVASIONS BY PEOPLE WHO CAME FROM BEYOND THE MOUNTAINS TO THE WEST.

INVADERS AND CONQUERORS

c. 2000 BC: Harrapan civilization spread into Ganges valley.

c. 1500 BC: Aryan invasion.

c. 325 BC – c. 232 BC: The Mauryan empire became India's strongest state.

c. AD 320 – c. AD 550: The Gupta empire covered most of India.

1192: Islamic empire established in northern India, resulting in the creation of the Sultanate of Delhi in 1206.

1526: Moghul empire established from Afghanistan to Bihar.

1600: The British East India Company began trading in India.

1858: India became part of the British Empire.

1947: India became two independent nations, India and Pakistan.

1971: New state of Bangladesh is established

1972: State of Bangladesh internationally recognized

THE FIRST PEOPLE TO LIVE in the Ganges valley arrived there about 4000 years ago. They came from the valley of the Indus in what is now Pakistan. There they had set up a civilization that is now known as the "Harappa" culture after the name of one of their main cities. The Harappan people moved to the upper Ganges and then eastwards along the river valley. Then, in about 1750 BC, the Harappan civilization ended. No one knows why, but some archaeologists believe that it may have been destroyed by a natural disaster such as an earthquake or floods.

THE ARYAN INFLUENCE

The next people to arrive on the Ganges were Aryans who came from central Asia. They farmed and bred horses and cattle, and in about 800 BC they discovered how to make iron tools. The Aryans created small kingdoms. Gradually these kingdoms began to fight among themselves. The kingdom of Maurya, with its capital at present-day Patna, took over the whole of northern India. After its great ruler Asoka died in 232 BC, the Mauryan empire

▶ *The Lahore Gate, the main entrance to the Red Fort in Delhi. The Red Fort was built for the Moghul emperor Shah Jahan, who ruled over most of India from 1627 to 1658. It was designed as the centerpiece of the new capital he built at Delhi.*

▶ *The Jami Masjid mosque at Fatehpur Sikri was designed to hold 10,000 Muslim worshippers. Thousands of childless women, Muslim and Hindu, come to the mosque each year to pray for a son.*

THE GHOST CITY OF FATEHPUR SIKRI

The Moghul emperor Akbar chose to build his capital on the top of a hill 23 miles (37 kilometers) south-west of Agra on the Yamuna, overlooking the Ganges plain. He founded the city in 1569 and lived there in great splendor until his death in 1602. Within 50 years, Fatehpur Sikri was deserted. But its ruins, protected by massive walls, have been partly restored to remind visitors of what was for 30 years the richest and most colorful city in India.

broke up. Northern India was again invaded by people from the east, who were attracted by the rich soil of the Ganges.

The next great empire to emerge was the Gupta empire, which lasted for about 200 years until the sixth century AD. The Guptas were the first Indian rulers to develop trade both within their empire and outside. But again this empire collapsed when more invaders arrived from the east.

Raiders continued to attack northern India over the years, but the next serious invasion was in the tenth century AD when Islamic troops marched across the mountains. They slowly advanced down the Ganges until, by 1206, they controlled most of the valley. They called their kingdom the "Sultanate of Delhi." The Sultanate lasted for over 200 years, but it grew weaker and in 1523 northern India faced yet another invasion, by the Moghuls from Persia. It was during the reign of the Moghuls, which lasted for nearly 200 years, that many of India's great palaces and fortresses were built. By 1707 many Moghul princes decided to rule their own states, and the Moghul empire began to disintegrate.

THE ARRIVAL OF THE EUROPEANS

Merchants from Portugal, France, Great Britain, Holland and Denmark began to open up trade between India and Europe in about 1500. Great Britain became the most powerful of these trading nations, and in 1858 India – which at this time also included Pakistan and Bangladesh – became part of the British Empire. However, in many places, Moghul princes continued to rule their territories as part of the British Empire until India became independent in 1947.

BELIEFS AND BELIEVERS

THE GANGES IS THE "HOLY RIVER" OF HINDUISM. EVERY HINDU, HOWEVER POOR, HOPES ONE DAY TO VISIT THE GANGES AND BATHE IN ITS WATER.

HINDUISM is the religion of 85 per cent of Indian people. Some Hindu beliefs come from the Harappa people of the Indus valley. Others come from the Aryans who followed them. It is not surprising that the Ganges came to be worshiped. To the first settlers along its banks, its annual flood, which provided rich soil for their crops, must have seemed like a miracle. They depended on the river for their lives. Hinduism has many gods, some worshiped only by people of one family or village, but the Ganges is worshiped by all.

▲ *The temple at Badrinath, in the foothills of the Himalayas about 31 miles (50 kilometers) from the Gangotri glacier, is visited by Hindu and Buddhist pilgrims.*

One of the beliefs of Hinduism is that every family belongs to a group called a *jati*, or caste. Their caste determines what kind of work they can do, whom they can marry, and who their friends are. Despite attempts to do away with the caste system, it is still important in the lives of Hindus, especially in rural areas.

THE ISLAMIC INFLUENCE

The invaders who came to northern India in the tenth century AD brought with them their own religion, Islam. This religion is based on the teachings of Mohammed, and it was written down by his followers after his death in the year 632. Followers of Islam are called Muslims. Some Muslim rulers in India frightened Hindus into changing their beliefs, or made them pay special taxes. Others, such

▲ *Muslim women, wearing the traditional chador which covers them from head to foot, go shopping in a trishaw, the modern version of the Indian rickshaw.*

▲ *A statue of Buddha. He is usually shown in this position, as it is the position used by Buddhists when meditating.*

as the Moghul emperor Akbar who ruled India from 1556 to 1605, encouraged the two groups of believers to live together in peace. Akbar even married a Hindu princess. But the history of the Indian subcontinent has been one of distrust between Hindus and Muslims, which still continues today.

BUDDHISTS AND SIKHS

Two of India's other religions sprang from Hinduism. Buddhism was founded about 2500 years ago by a Hindu prince, Siddhartha, who was brought up in what is now Nepal. He called himself the Buddha, meaning "one who has found the truth." Buddhists spend part of each day in meditation – a time of quiet thinking about what life means.

Another young Hindu was the founder of a new religion. He was Nanak and was born in northwestern India in 1469. As he grew up, he began to question Hindu beliefs and welcomed people of any religion who came to listen to him. He called his followers "sikhs," and Sikhism became the name of the religion he led.

RELIGION IN INDIA AND BANGLADESH
INDIA (population 1996: 953 million)
Hindus: 762 million
Muslims: 133 million
Buddhists: 6.6 million
Sikhs: 19 million
Christians: 23 million
Other/none: 10 million
BANGLADESH (population 1996: 131 million)
Hindus: 21 million
Muslims: 108.5 million
Other/none: 1.5 million

DIFFERENT WAYS OF LIFE

In India, religious belief rules everyday life. Each religion has its own ways of worship, feast days and festivals. The Ganges itself is important only to Hindus, but many people have settled in the valley over the centuries, bringing their beliefs with them. Many Buddhist and Islamic holy places share the banks of the river.

▲ *At sunset, Hindu pilgrims float lighted candles on the Ganges at Varanasi as they offer prayers to the river-goddess Ganga.*

INDIA AND BANGLADESH

THE GANGES FLOWS THROUGH TWO COUNTRIES. MOST OF ITS COURSE RUNS ACROSS NORTHERN INDIA, BUT FOR ITS LAST 311 MILES (500 KILOMETERS) IT FLOWS THROUGH BANGLADESH AND IS CALLED THE PADMA.

FROM 1838 TO 1947, THE WHOLE OF the Indian subcontinent was part of the British Empire, but in August 1947 India became independent. The subcontinent was split into two separate states – India for the Hindus and Pakistan for the Muslims. Pakistan was made up of two regions. The country we call Pakistan today, with its capital at Islamabad, was called West Pakistan. East Pakistan, on the delta of the Ganges and the Brahmaputra, was present-day Bangladesh with Dhaka as its capital. The two regions were 994 miles (1600 kilometers) away from each other, separated by India. Today, it is hard to believe that anyone thought that such a divided country could be governed effectively as one.

▲ *December 1971: Sheikh Mujibar Rahman (holding up a shield) rides in triumph through the streets of Dhaka after Bangladesh becomes an independent nation.*

VIOLENCE AND BLOODSHED

Of course, it was not possible to divide up the population by drawing borders on a map so that all the Hindus lived in one country and all the Muslims in the other. As the day of independence drew near, five million Sikhs and Hindus began to move from the new Pakistan to the new India and five million Muslims moved in the opposite direction.

When the crowds of refugees met, there was violence and bloodshed. More than one million people died. But most people stayed put. Today, there are 133 million Muslims living in the Hindu state of India and 21 million Hindus in the Islamic state of Bangladesh.

CONTINUING WARS

Creating two separate states did not lead to peace. India and Pakistan quarreled over the state of Kashmir on their northern borders. Both countries wanted it, but most Kashmiris were Muslim. Meanwhile, there were quarrels

between East Pakistan and West Pakistan. West Pakistan was the more prosperous of the two. The leaders who controlled the government and the army came from West Pakistan, although East Pakistan had the larger population. In March 1971, civil war broke out between the two regions. The powerful Pakistan army swept into East Pakistan and killed thousands of people. In December, the even more powerful Indian army moved in to stop the killing.

In January 1972 East Pakistan became an independent nation with the new name of Bangladesh. But independence cost the lives of about one million people. About ten million refugees from Bangladesh fled into India, where they had to find new homes and rebuild their lives.

CROWDED BANGLADESH

Bangladesh is the most densely-populated country in the world. In 1996 there were 351 people to each square mile (909 people to each square kilometer) of land. This compares with 115 people to each square mile (300 people per square kilometer) in India, 91 in the United Kingdom (sq mi) and 10 in the United States (sq mi).

▶ *Victims of the fight for Bangladeshi independence. A family of refugees, fleeing from the war, make their way across the border to Calcutta.*

TALES OF THE GANGES

HINDUS BELIEVE THAT ALL THE WATER ON EARTH CAME FROM THE GANGA, OR GANGES. THROUGHOUT HISTORY THE GANGES HAS BEEN IMPORTANT IN THE LIVES OF WORSHIPERS, WARRIORS AND LANDOWNERS.

THE ANGRY GANGES

HINDUS BELIEVE that in the beginning of time the river-goddess, Ganga, flowed through heaven, and Earth had no water at all. King Bhagirathi, who ruled over the land around the mountain stream that is named after him today, was worried that life on Earth would be destroyed unless there was water.

The king prayed for many years to the Hindu god Shiva, the god of life, to send Ganga to Earth. When Shiva told Ganga about this,

▲ *Shiva, the Hindu god of life, stands at the meeting of the Bhagirathi and Alaknanda rivers that join to form the Ganges at Deoprayag. Beside him is the elephant-headed Ganesh, the god of success and good fortune, and behind his head is the river-goddess Ganga.*

◀ *One of the many hundreds of shrines dedicated to the river-goddess Ganga at Varanasi on the banks of the Ganges. Pilgrims leave gifts of garlands, metalware and food in return for the gift of Ganga's river.*

she was angry. She threatened to jump to Earth with such violence that she would set it spinning and drown everything on it. Shiva went away to pray at the top of his favorite mountain in the Himalayas, above the Gangotri glacier. Sure enough, Ganga carried out her threat and threw herself at the Earth. But Shiva took the full weight of Ganga on his head. Ganga's water caught in his hair, where it flowed for seven years trying to find a way out. At last, it flowed from the Himalayas in seven streams – one of them called the Bhagirathi – which came together to form the Ganges river.

ASOKA'S EMPIRE

One of the greatest rulers the Indian sub-continent ever had was Asoka, who became king of the Mauryan Empire in 272 BC. The Mauryan Empire stretched westwards along the Ganges valley from its capital at Patna. When he became king, Asoka set out to conquer the whole of India. In 261 BC, he attacked the kingdom of Kalinga on India's eastern coast. Over 100,000 people were killed. The slaughter so shocked Asoka that he decided to give up war and become a Buddhist. An important Buddhist belief is that it is wrong to kill any living thing.

For the next 30 years, Asoka ruled over a peaceful empire in which the poor, elderly and sick were looked after. He built wells to bring water to villages that had none and reservoirs to store water for the dry season.

Asoka was also a good friend to travelers. Among the roads he built across his empire was the Royal Highway. This ran westwards along the Ganges valley from Patna to Hardwar. Then it went on to Peshawar, now on the border between Pakistan and Afghanistan. The Royal Highway was lined with trees to give shade for travelers and their animals, and there were rest-houses for them to shelter in overnight. The Royal Highway still exists, though nowadays it is called the Grand Trunk Road and is busier and less comfortable to travel upon than in Asoka's time.

THE MAHARAJAH'S URNS

Under British rule, the state of Jaipur in northwestern India was governed by a Maharajah who was a devout Hindu. In 1902 he was invited to London to see Edward VII crowned as ruler of the British Empire. The only water the Maharajah would drink was from the Ganges. When he set out by sea for London, he took with him enough Ganges water to last for the entire six months of the trip. It was stored in two huge silver urns, which are said to be the largest ever made. The Maharajah's palace in the city of Jaipur is now a museum, where the two silver urns can still be seen.

OUT OF THE MOUNTAINS

THE STREAMS THAT MAKE UP THE GANGES BEGIN THEIR JOURNEY AMONG THE PEAKS AND GLACIERS OF THE HIMALAYAS, THE HIGHEST MOUNTAIN RANGE ON EARTH.

▲ *Near the Gangotri glacier, a Hindu pilgrim bathes in the icy water of the Bhagirathi. He is a Sadhu, a Hindu "wise man" who spends his life in prayer.*

THE LONGEST OF THESE STREAMS is the Bhagirathi. This stream begins life as meltwater from the Gangotri glacier, which is over 13,943 feet (4250 meters) above sea level. The village about 12 miles (20 kilometers) below the glacier, also called Gangotri, is an important place of pilgrimage for Hindus. They bathe in the Bhagirathi and worship at the temple dedicated to the river-goddess Ganga.

WATERFALLS AND CANYONS

The Bhagirathi is joined by other streams as it tumbles over waterfalls and rapids, gathers in deep pools and cuts through narrow canyons on its way down the mountains. In the spring, when melting snow swells the waters, and again in the summer when the monsoon reaches the mountains, the streams turn into rushing torrents.

The largest stream is the Alaknanda, which meets the Bhagirathi at the village of Deoprayag. This is another holy place. Steps have been cut in the rocks to allow pilgrims to go down to the river to bathe. From Deoprayag onwards, the combined streams take the name Ganges or Ganga.

▼ *The meeting of the Bhagirathi and Alaknanda rivers at Deoprayag. The pilgrims' bathing-place, or ghat, is in the center. On the left, partly hidden by trees, is a footbridge that connects the old town, in the picture, with an area of more modern buildings.*

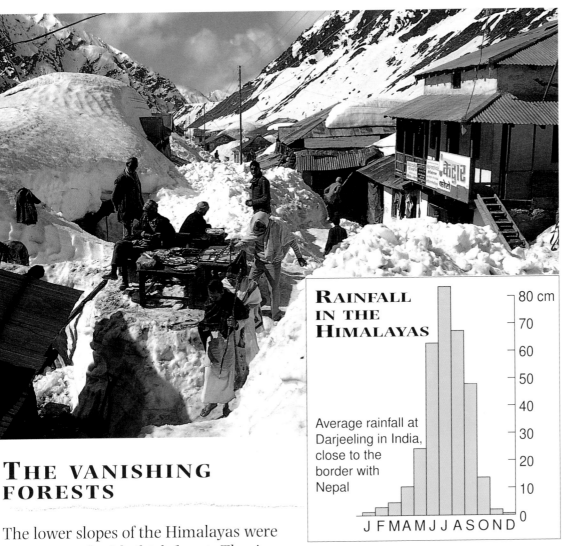

◀ *A party of pilgrims on their way to Kedarnath, another Hindu pilgrimage site close to the Gangotri glacier. The route, along tracks over 984 feet (3000 meters) high, is snow-bound and closed to tourists from November to May. This does not deter the devout Hindu pilgrims.*

RAINFALL IN THE HIMALAYAS

Average rainfall at Darjeeling in India, close to the border with Nepal

80 cm
70
60
50
40
30
20
10
0

J F M A M J J A S O N D

THE VANISHING FORESTS

The lower slopes of the Himalayas were once covered with thick forest. The Aryan invaders of northwestern India began to clear this for farming 3500 years ago. When, in about 1000 BC, they discovered how to make iron, the pace of forest clearance increased. Wood was needed for the fires in which iron was made, and, in turn, iron axes made the felling of trees easier. But the effect on the forests of people using hand tools was tiny compared with the damage that has been done in the past 50 years by workers with modern machinery. The wood was needed for building and the cleared land was needed to grow food for the increasing population of Nepal. Many of the Ganges' tributaries begin in Nepal and over half the forests have been cleared there since the 1950s. Few trees are replaced with new young ones. The result is that with no covering of vegetation to absorb the heavy rains, and no roots to help hold the soil in

place, millions of tons of soil are washed off the land into the rivers and eventually find their way into the Ganges. This raises the water level in the valley and increases the likelihood of flooding. This loss of soil is called "soil erosion."

REMOTE COUNTRY

The mountains are very thinly populated. Hill farmers live there and they rely on yaks for transport as well as for milk, meat and leather. There are a few isolated villages on the hillsides. Goods are sold or bartered at the markets and people make a living from pilgrims and other visitors. Transport along the narrow, unmade roads is slow and dangerous, and some villages can be reached only by yak or mule, or on foot.

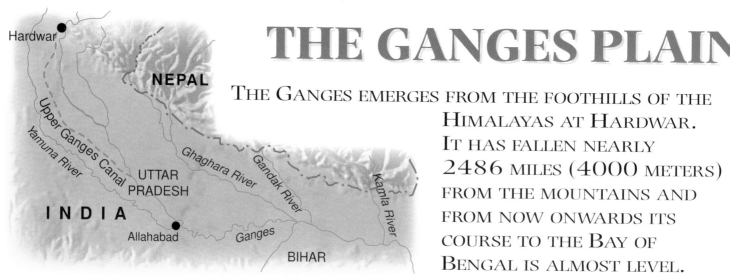

THE GANGES PLAIN

THE GANGES EMERGES FROM THE FOOTHILLS OF THE HIMALAYAS AT HARDWAR. IT HAS FALLEN NEARLY 2486 MILES (4000 METERS) FROM THE MOUNTAINS AND FROM NOW ONWARDS ITS COURSE TO THE BAY OF BENGAL IS ALMOST LEVEL.

HARDWAR STANDS AT THE HEAD of the great Ganges plain, which stretches across northern India for over 746 miles (1200 kilometers) through the states of Uttar Pradesh and Bihar. The plain is between 186 and 249 miles (300 and 400 kilometers) wide and across it flows not only the Ganges but several other rivers whose sources are in the Himalayas. The largest of these is the Yamuna, which rises in the mountains to the west of Gangotri glacier and flows for 854 miles (1375 kilometers) parallel to the Ganges until it joins the main river at Allahabad.

The state of Uttar Pradesh, which covers the western half of the Ganges plain, is India's most heavily populated region. Over 150 million people live there, with an average of 200 people per square mile (518 people per square kilometer). (By contrast, California, which is the USA's most heavily populated state, has 24 people to a square mile [62 people to a square kilometer]. Most of them live in small villages and earn their living from farming (see pages 24-25).

▼ *The Ganges at Allahabad. The city is almost hidden in mist in the far distance. On the right is the Yamuna river.*

THE MONSOON

The Ganges plain owes its rich soil to the river and the climate. The river provides the sediment from the mountains. The climate provides the monsoon. The rainy season arrives on the plain in June and finishes in September when it moves north. Before June there are two months of fierce, dry heat. The dry, hot air rises and moves north over the Himalayas. Tropical rainstorms sweep in from the Indian Ocean and moist air from the rain fills the gap left by the rising hot air.

The amount of rain the monsoon brings can vary from year to year, especially in Uttar Pradesh where it arrives last. During some years there is enough water to break the river banks and destroy whole villages. In other years, the monsoon fails and the crops that depend on it shrivel, resulting in food shortages. Some scientists believe that failure of the monsoon to bring rain is becoming more frequent.

THE UPPER GANGES CANAL

Until about 150 years ago, the Ganges in Uttar Pradesh often changed its course when it flooded, leaving farmland on its regular course dry. Crops died. In 1845 a huge irrigation plan, the Upper Ganges Canal, was begun. A dam was built at Hardwar to divert most of the Ganges water and send it along about 559 miles (900 kilometers) of irrigation channels. This ensured that land on each side of the canals was permanently watered. Since then, the plan has been extended to irrigate more land, and the dam now includes a hydroelectric power station. The Canal acts as a store for any surplus water that falls in the monsoon, so that it can be released later to make the growing season longer.

GLOBAL WARMING

Many scientists believe that the Earth's climate is changing. By studying weather records throughout the world they have found out that average temperatures are half a degree Celsius higher than they were in 1900. This rise in temperature is altering the world's weather pattern. The last serious failure of the monsoon in India was in 1987, when nearly 200 million people faced food shortages. But this was one of six years in the 1980s when monsoon rainfall was less than normal, and the pattern has continued into the 1990s.

◄ These multi-storey buildings along the banks of the Upper Ganges Canal at Hardwar are pilgrims' hostels. Pilgrims use them when making pilgrimages to the sacred sites.

VILLAGES ON THE PLAIN

THE GANGES PLAIN IS MAINLY AN AREA OF SMALL VILLAGES.
CLUSTERS OF HOUSES BUILT OF BAKED MUD OR BRICK ARE
SURROUNDED BY LAND THAT THE VILLAGERS FARM.

COMPARED WITH FARMS in Europe or America, Indian farms are tiny. Three-quarters of Indian farmers own less than five acres (two hectares) of land, which is about the size of two football fields. These farms may have to support a large family, consisting of grandparents, parents and children. Many of these families can only grow enough food for themselves. This is known as subsistence farming. Others rent more land, often at very high prices, from other landowners. Many families could not survive without money sent home by sons or daughters who have moved away to work in the cities or to other parts of the world. Others have to borrow money to rent land, to buy seeds and tools, or perhaps to build a well. Farmers can build up huge debts that have to be paid out of their small incomes.

▼ *Farming families often turn to other ways of making a living. This boy's clay pots will be sold at the village market.*

▲ *An island near Kanpur. It is flooded when the monsoon comes, but in the dry season it is used for crops. The young plants are protected from the wind by windbreaks.*

TEACHING BY TELEVISION

The Indian government relies on television to take information to rural areas like the Ganges plain, where less than half the population can read. Few poor farming families have their own televisions, but they gather to watch the programs in schools and village halls. The government uses television to pass on information about farming methods, health, looking after children and limiting the size of families.

THE GREEN REVOLUTION

Despite these problems, India is able to feed itself better than 50 years ago. Between 1947 and 1996 the amount of grain produced, mainly rice and wheat, increased by almost four times. Part of this increase was due to irrigation plans, but most was the result of the "Green Revolution." Scientists in Mexico and the Philippines bred new varieties of grain seeds which produced higher yields from each plant. Farmers have to use chemicals to make the soil richer and to kill insects that damage the crops in order to obtain higher yields. With help from the United Nations, the Green Revolution began to show results in India and Pakistan in about 1970.

Although the Green Revolution has put an end to the food shortages that once plagued India, it has not helped the poorer farmers much. The cost of Green Revolution farming is high. For example, a pair of oxen can be fed on waste from farm crops, but a tractor needs fuel and spare parts that have to be bought from suppliers. Therefore many small farmers on the Ganges plain stick to their old methods of cultivation despite attempts by the Indian government to persuade them to change.

LEAVING THE VILLAGES

Most people on the Ganges plain will spend all their lives in their own village or, if they are women and they marry, a neighboring one. In the past, sons stayed at home and worked on the farm. When a farmer died, his land was divided among his sons. This meant that farms became smaller with each generation. Today, this kind of future is not good enough for many young people. They move away to the cities to find work or to go to college. Although they leave the villages, they never leave their families. The family may have borrowed money to pay for their education, but this will be paid back many times over when the young people start working.

CITIES OF THE PLAIN

THE MOST IMPORTANT CITIES OF THE GANGES PLAIN ARE
EITHER ON THE GANGES ITSELF OR ON ITS MAJOR TRIBUTARY,
THE YAMUNA, WHICH JOINS THE GANGES AT ALLAHABAD.

BY FAR THE LARGEST CITY on the upper Ganges
is Kanpur, on the southern bank of the river.
It is a city of factories and textile mills with a
population of over two million.

When Britain ruled India, Kanpur was
chosen as an army base and workshops there
began making harnesses for army horses.
Kanpur's major industry, making leather
goods of all kinds, grew from this. Cotton and
wool are also spun and woven at Kanpur, but
the mills are over 100 years old and their
machinery is old-fashioned. People investing
money in industry prefer to put it into new
factories rather than modernize old ones,
and so Kanpur's textile industries are slowly
declining.

▲ *The Secretariat Buildings in New Delhi, built in
the 1920s as offices from which the British ruled
India. The buildings contain over 1000 rooms
where Indian government officials now work.*

THE MEETING
OF RIVERS

The Ganges and the Yamuna meet at
Allahabad. Hindus believe that they are
joined there by a third underground river,
the Saraswati, and so Allahabad is a place of
pilgrimage each spring. Allahabad also has an
Islamic history. The name, given to it by the
Moghul emperor Akbar, means "City of God."
The fort he built there in 1583 can still be seen.

▲ *A very different scene in New Delhi. On the edge of the overcrowded city, a woman collects water from the polluted Yamuna river.*

PEOPLE IN THE CITIES

Although every Indian city has its slums, life for most city people is better than for people in the country. Industry pays better wages than farming, and the cities provide work for professional people such as doctors, nurses, lawyers and teachers. In farming villages, women have few chances to improve their lives. Daughters who move to the cities to find work in the professions discover that, for the first time, they have the same opportunities as men.

Modern Allahabad is a city with a population of over 800,000. The position of the city is important. In the middle of the Ganges plain, and with good road and rail links to the east, west and south, it is a marketing center for the plain's farm produce. Its main industries are food processing and cotton manufacture.

INDIA'S CAPITAL

In Delhi, on the Yamuna, India is governed from a set of splendid buildings designed and built 70 years ago. The area, called New Delhi, is landscaped with ornamental pools and fountains, gardens and tree-lined avenues.

New Delhi, with its population of government officials, business people and national leaders, is very different from Old Delhi about two miles (three kilometers) away. Old Delhi is a trading city and its narrow streets are filled with stalls and workshops selling everything from spices and fruit to clothes and jewelery. Craftspeople often live and work in the rooms above their shops.

The growing population of Delhi – 6.5 million, and expected to double by 2001 – worries the Indian government. Delhi is a magnet for poor people from the villages who are looking for work. The government is trying to take the pressure off Delhi by creating "counter-magnets" – new cities with new industries. Faridabad, 18 miles (30 kilometers) south of Delhi, is one example. Twenty years ago it was a tiny village. Today it is a city of 500,000 people, with engineering, glass-making, chemical and electrical goods industries.

▲ *At Agra, dhobis – washermen – wash clothes in the Yamuna river. Washing clothes is "low caste" work, and Indians who do it have little contact with people of other castes. The result is that the business stays in dhobi families.*

VARANASI

To Hindus, the most important city on the Ganges is Varanasi, "the City of Light."

◀ *The Dasashwamedh Ghat, the largest of 70 bathing-places along the Ganges at Varanasi. Some pilgrims bathe from the steps, but others hire boats to take them out to the middle of the river.*

HINDUS BELIEVE THAT VARANASI was the place chosen by Shiva, the god of life, as his home after he married the goddess Parvati. Pilgrims have been visiting Varanasi for over 3000 years. It is the center of Hindu religion and learning, with a large Hindu University, founded in 1898, on the sacred left bank of the river at the edge of the city. Just as all Muslims hope to visit their holy city, Mecca in Saudi Arabia, once in their lives, it is the aim of all Hindus to visit Varanasi to bathe in the Ganges. This, they believe, will wash away anything wrong they have done during their lives. Many hope to die there, be cremated and have their ashes scattered on the river.

HINDU PILGRIMS

One million people live in Varanasi, but millions more visit the city each year as pilgrims. Some make the journey on foot, even from the most distant parts of India, but most these days travel by road or rail. There are over 1500 shrines and temples in the city streets and along the riverside where they can say their prayers. They head for the ghats, or sets of steps, which line the west bank of the Ganges for about 3 miles (five kilometers). There, they bathe in the river and the women throw posies of flowers on the water. Others stand on the steps and wash their clothes, or pay someone to do it. The river bank is busy with traders hiring out boats and umbrellas and selling holy souvenirs and refreshments. Between the ghats there are two places that have been set aside for cremation. Bodies are burned to ashes over pyres, or fires, of sandalwood and straw.

WORKSHOPS AND WEAVERS

Providing food and rooms for Hindu pilgrims, and for thousands of non-Hindu visitors who go to Varanasi each year to experience its colorful life, is the city's major industry. There are comfortable hotels and less expensive

◄ *The Manikarnika Ghat at Varanasi, where Hindus burn the bodies of their relatives, after washing them in the Ganges, on funeral pyres built of sweet-smelling sandalwood.*

▼ *At dawn, the ghats of Varanasi come alive when pilgrims, Hindu priests, fortune-tellers and sellers of food and holy Ganges water arrive. They leave at sunset.*

VARANASI'S SUMMER

Floods are an annual feature of life in Varanasi when the monsoon rains come in mid-June and the level of the Ganges rises. Many small businesses close down, and people who have moved to Varanasi from the villages of the plains return home for a few weeks to work in the fields. When the water level drops again in September, the hectic life of the "City of Light" begins again.

places to stay. Many pilgrims camp out in the open wherever they can find room, either cooking their own food or buying it from stalls in the streets.

Varanasi is also a center of the Indian silk industry. It is famous all over the world for its rich silk fabrics and brocade – silk material containing gold or silver threads woven into rich patterns. These were once woven by hand in small family workshops, but today there are large factories producing great quantities of material for world markets. Other important industries in Varanasi include toy-making, jewelery and brass metalwork.

BUDDHIST VARANASI

Varanasi is also important to Buddhists. It was at Sarnath, only 6 miles (ten kilometers) north of the city, that Siddhartha, the Buddha, preached for the first time around 500 BC. According to his followers, he had been wandering through India trying to find an answer to the question of why so many people lived such unhappy lives. At Sarnath, he rested from the sun under a wild fig tree, and it was there that he worked out "the truth." This was that everyone, however unhappy or poor, could find happiness by aiming to live a good life.

CALCUTTA

AS THE GANGES FLOWS FROM INDIA INTO BANGLADESH, A BRANCH BREAKS AWAY SOUTHWARDS, TAKING A SHORT CUT TO THE BAY OF BENGAL. THIS IS THE HOOGHLY RIVER. TOWARDS ITS SOUTHERN END IS THE CITY OF CALCUTTA.

◀ *A family in Rambagan, one of Calcutta's "bustees," or slum areas. Many such families make a living by searching the city's garbage dumps for things that they can mend, clean up and sell. The lane between the houses, which is an open drain, is a hazard to health and a source of disease.*

CALCUTTA, with 12 million people, is India's largest city. It is 96 miles (154 kilometers) upriver from the Bay of Bengal and for 250 years it has been India's main trading port with the outside world. For 80 years, until 1912, it was India's capital. The manufacture and export of jute – a plant fiber used to make sacks and rope – was its main industry. In the past 50 years, artificial fibers have taken over many of the old uses of jute, but there are still 60 jute factories at work in Calcutta.

Calcutta has also had to overcome the threat to its shipping trade caused by the increasing size of ocean-going ships that could not use the narrow and shallow Hooghly river. A new port has been built at Haldia, 40 miles (64 kilometers) lower down the Hooghly, which can take large container ships and oil tankers.

OVERCROWDED CITY

In the partition of India in 1947, the Ganges delta to the east of Calcutta became East Pakistan. Hindu refugees from the new Islamic state poured across the border, seeking homes and work. There was another flood of refugees in 1971 when Bangladesh became an independent country. Every day, hundreds of people still arrive in Calcutta from Bangladesh and from other parts of India. Today, it is a very overcrowded city where 150,000 people have nowhere to sleep except on the streets. Hundreds of thousands of other families live in crowded conditions in the "bustees," with only one room for a family. Calcutta's run-down slum areas. Even in the center of the city bamboo huts with roofs made of plastic or sacking have been built on waste ground, where people try to earn a living by sorting rags and other waste. There is not enough electricity to supply the city and power cuts or "brown-outs" – when the lights go dim and machinery slows down – often occur. Calcutta's streets are choked with all sorts of traffic – lorries, cars, scooters, bicycles, rickshaws and bullock carts – as well as people on foot.

MOTHER TERESA

The sad plight of Calcutta's street-dwellers, especially their children, led a Roman Catholic nun from Albania, Mother Teresa, to start work among them in 1953. Under her leadership, hospitals and children's homes were opened, and her helpers took food, clothes and medicine to people in the streets. The movement she founded, the Missionaries of Charity, spread all over India and to 25 other countries, but Mother Teresa remained in Calcutta among the people she had first helped. In 1979 she was awarded the Nobel Peace Prize.

▶ *Traffic of all kinds mingles in one of Calcutta's main streets: cars, taxis, delivery vans, rickshaws and farmers carrying their produce to market on their heads. The rails in the road are reminders of Calcutta's streetcar system, now replaced by an underground subway.*

PROBLEM CITY

The United Nations' World Bank has recognized Calcutta as one of the world's problem cities, which needs more help than the Indian government can afford. In 1986 the first sections of a long-planned underground subway were opened to take pedestrians off the streets. In 1992 a second bridge across the Hooghly was opened to ease traffic on the Howrah bridge, the only other crossing. But Calcutta needs more than underground subways and bridges. The bustees, with few or no supplies of drinking water and poor drainage systems to carry away waste, are breeding-grounds for disease. The city's government has cleared some of the worst areas, but Calcutta's problems are so huge that it is difficult to see an end to them.

THE GANGES DELTA

THE DELTA OF THE GANGES, WHERE THE RIVER CROSSES 311 MILES (500 KILOMETERS) OF SILT AND SWAMP TO REACH THE SEA, IS THE LARGEST RIVER DELTA IN THE WORLD.

THE DELTA COVERS 50,190 square miles (130,000 square kilometers) – an area the size of England. It is made up of silt. Rocks have been ground down into mud by the action of the Ganges, the Brahmaputra and their tributaries, and have been carried down the rivers over thousands of years.

The Ganges and the Brahmaputra, which flows from the north, meet about 12 miles (20 kilometers) north of Faridpur. The combined river is called the "Padma." More silt is brought down to the delta by a third river, the Meghna, which flows in from the northeast.

Although the Padma carries most of the water of the two rivers to the sea, a maze of smaller rivers take some of it. These change

▲ *Farmers on the delta in Bangladesh collect silt. They spread it above the flood level to make the land more fertile.*

▲ TOP: *These houses at Dhaka are built on stilts to keep them clear of floodwater. But the flimsy buildings offer no protection against cyclones which sometimes sweep across the delta. This happened in 1991, killing 200,000 people and making millions homeless.*

their courses with the seasons and from year to year, forming islands of silt. Around the main mouth of the Padma, in southeast Bangladesh, people live on and farm these islands, called "chars." Some of the chars are often less than three feet (a meter) above high tide.

THE SUNDARBANS

The Padma meets the sea across a strip of swamp called the "Sundarbans." It runs for about 168 miles (270 kilometers) along the

▼ *A farming family on the Sundarbans threshes the rice crop. The rice stalks are beaten over the metal grid to separate the grains. The stalks will be used as cattle-feed.*

▼ *Fishermen work at their nets in one of the waterways of the Ganges delta.*

coast and stretches back about 62 miles (100 kilometers) inland. The name comes from the "sundari" tree, a tropical hardwood that once covered the area. Sundari wood makes good building timber and most of the trees have now been chopped down. Today, the Sundarbans are muddy islands covered with gewa – a softwood used for paper-making – bamboo and tangled, twisting mangroves.

CROWDED BANGLADESH

Almost all of the delta is in Bangladesh, one of the most densely populated and least developed countries in the world. Bangladesh has a population of 131 million. If it continues to grow at the present rate, it will have reached 200 million by the year 2020. Eighty per cent of Bangladeshis live in villages. The main cities are the capital Dhaka, its nearby river port Narayanganj, Khulna, on the delta, and Bangladesh's main port, Chittagong, on the east side of the Bay of Bengal.

Bangladesh is the world's largest producer of jute, which is used to make burlap and sacking. Rice-growing for its own population is Bangladesh's most important activity, but in the 1990s farmers have begun to grow a wider variety of crops for export. The soil and climate are good for luxury crops such as asparagus and mangoes, which are sold in the Middle East and eastern Asia. This export trade brings in foreign currency, which enables Bangladesh to buy farming machinery and other manufactured goods from abroad. About half of Bangladesh's export earnings come from people who have gone to work in Europe and the Middle East and send money home to their families.

THE FISHING INDUSTRY

The rivers and channels of the delta support a thriving fishing industry. Fish breed in the rivers and are caught when the monsoon floodwater rises. Some Bangladeshi fishermen use trained otters to behave rather like sheepdogs, swimming underwater and driving schools of fish into the nets. Over 75 per cent of the delta catch is freshwater fish, which is a vital part of the Bangladeshi diet. But in the past fifteen years sea fishermen have built up an export trade in shrimp and other seafood, which are exported to Japan, Europe and the USA.

PEOPLE OF THE DELTA

THE CLIMATE OF THE GANGES DELTA MAKES IT GOOD FARMING LAND. BUT IT CAN ALSO BRING DEATH AND DESTRUCTION.

FARMERS ON THE DELTA need the annual monsoon rain to water their crops and to wash away the salt that seeps into the delta from the sea. When the floods go, they leave behind a new layer of rich silt. But in a bad year they can also leave behind ruined villages and fields that have been washed away.

There is another danger on the delta. Cyclones are fierce storms that sweep in from the Bay of Bengal, which can bring tidal waves with them. In 1991 nearly 200,000 people were drowned on the delta when villages on the char islands were swept away by cyclone floods.

LIFE IN THE VILLAGES

The people who live on the Ganges delta in Bangladesh are among the poorest in the world. Most of them live in 65,000 farming villages, in houses with mud or woven bamboo walls and straw roofs. Often three or even four generations of a family live in one house, sleeping on mats on the floor. In order to cook they burn dried animal droppings, straw and rice husks. There is no water supply apart from the creeks and irrigation channels of the delta, in which they also wash themselves and their animals.

THE MONSOON
From June to September each year, monsoon winds from the south bring heavy rain to the Ganges delta. An average of 9 inches (24 centimeters) of rain falls in each of these months, normally flooding about 20 per cent of the delta. But in some monsoon seasons the winds are so strong that they cause sea water to surge up against the flow of the river. This tidal surge can cover 80 per cent of the delta with water.

▲ *Survivors clear up the damage after the cyclone of 1991. Since then, the Bangladeshi government has started a program of building cyclone shelters that will save lives but not homes or crops.*

▶ *In a Western country, floods like this would be treated as a disaster. But in Bangladesh minor floods of this kind are welcomed because they deposit a fresh layer of silt that will enrich the fields.*

◄ *Fish swim in the flooded paddy-fields where rice is growing. They provide a useful extra source of food. This woman uses a long bamboo rod as she stands on the road.*

▲ *Harvesting the jute crop. Farmers dive under the water to cut the stalks, which are left to dry until the bark falls away. The plant fibers, which are about .08 inches (two millimeters) thick, can then be separated and sorted.*

About half of the farming families own at least some of the land they farm, but the farms are small. Quite often, they are made up of small pieces of land scattered around the village, which makes plowing and looking after the crops more difficult. Only five per cent of Bangladeshi farms cover more than 7 acres (three hectares), which is less than the area of three football fields. The main crop is rice.

Today most Bangladeshi farming people are better fed than only a generation ago. Only 30 years ago, farmers thought they were lucky if they managed to grow enough rice for their own families. Today, with better irrigation, better seeds and the use of fertilizers, 2.5 acres (one hectare) of land grows enough rice to feed a family. In most years there is a surplus of rice that the farmer can sell.

LIFE ON THE WATER

There are few roads on the delta, and many villages can be reached only by boat. River transport for farm produce as well as passengers is vital, and there are over 300,000 boats on the delta's waterways. After farming, fishing is the next most important activity, providing work for over five million people. In the freshwater creeks they catch carp and salmon. There are crabs and turtles in the Sundarbans, and large fleets sail out into the Bay of Bengal to net saltwater fish.

VISITING THE GANGES

MILLIONS OF PEOPLE TRAVEL TO THE GANGES EACH YEAR TO EXPERIENCE THE HISTORY AND RELIGION OF THE INDIAN SUBCONTINENT

MANY OF THEM are internal tourists, which means that they are visiting the Ganges from other parts of India. They come to worship at the Hindu shrines along the river, at the Muslim mosques and at the sacred sites of Buddhists. The thousands of pilgrims provide a living for street-sellers. Not all the pilgrims are from India. Many other people from around the world are interested in Hindu and Buddhist ideas and travel to India to experience them. Hindus and Buddhists who live abroad also come to India as pilgrims.

▼ *A tourist boat on the Ganges at Varanasi, with a ghat in the background.*

THE MOGHUL PAST

Other visitors come to admire the historical buildings. The most magnificent of these date from the days of Moghul rule. They include the Red Fort at Agra, built by the emperor Akbar alongside the Yamuna river, and the Taj Mahal nearby, India's most famous building. Akbar's grandson, Shah Jahan, built it between 1631 and 1648 as the tomb of his wife Mumtaz. The Moghuls, who ruled India from 1526 to 1857, left behind many other forts, palaces and mosques in India and Bangladesh.

INDIAN RAILWAYS

India has one of the largest railway networks in the world. The system, covering 41,634 miles (67,000 kilometers), is the main means of passenger transport for both Indians and foreign visitors. Tourist services include the Rajdhani Express from Calcutta to Delhi and the luxurious "Palace on Wheels," which takes visitors on a seven-day tour of northwestern India, starting from Delhi.

THE GANGES

▼ *With a "mahout," or driver, in charge, elephant rides are popular with tourists.*

ACTIVE HOLIDAYS

Tourists from abroad bring in foreign currency that is particularly valuable to countries like India and Bangladesh. They need it to buy skills and technology from other parts of the world. India has been successful in developing ski resorts and trekking tours in the Himalayas around the upper streams of the Ganges. They have also developed watersports such as sailing and white-water rafting on the upper Ganges itself. Since 1975, the Indian government has opened 53 national parks and 247 smaller wildlife sanctuaries. The first was the Corbett National Park, which overlooks the Ganges plain about 62 miles (100 kilometers) from Hardwar. Some of India's national parks have become so popular that the number of visitors has had to be cut to avoid damage to the protected habitats of plant and animal life.

TOURISM IN BANGLADESH

Bangladesh has not yet built up its tourist industry, unlike India. However, in 1992 the National Tourism Council was established to promote its tourist attractions. Currently most of the 50,000 visitors from abroad each year come on business. People on vacation need a variety of places to stay and eat, and they want to travel about easily. Outside the main cities, there are few facilities. Tourists have also been put off by Bangladesh's history of natural disasters. For example, the 1991 floods caused huge damage at the beach resort of Cox's Bazar on the eastern side of the Bay of Bengal south of Chittagong. But it will probably not be long before tourists discover Bangladesh's historical Muslim and Buddhist buildings, the wildlife of the Sundarbans and the beautiful beaches east of the delta.

THE WILDLIFE OF THE GANGES

DESPITE CENTURIES OF DEFORESTATION AND HUNTING, THE GANGES AND ITS PLAIN STILL PROVIDE HOMES FOR A WIDE RANGE OF ANIMALS. BUT SADLY, MANY ARE UNDER THREAT.

THE ROYAL BENGAL TIGER

The Royal Bengal tiger, found only in India, is the largest surviving member of the cat family. Less than 100 years ago there were about 40,000, but by 1970 there were fewer than 2000 left. In 1972 the World Wide Fund for Nature and the Indian government set up Project Tiger, aimed at protecting the remaining animals and building up their numbers. Today, numbers have risen to about 4000, but the struggle to protect the tiger is not over. Poachers still hunt tigers illegally, and hungry tigers still sometimes threaten Indian villages and so they are shot. In 1997 the Indian government announced new research into methods of protecting the Bengal tiger and increasing its numbers.

FOR 400 YEARS, Moghul and later British "big game" hunters slaughtered thousands of India's large animals, including lions, tigers, cheetahs and leopards, for sport. Hunting went on until about 50 years ago. Hunters today carry cameras instead of guns, but poachers still poison or trap large animals such as tigers and rhinoceros. They sell the skins, and the bones are ground down to powder and sent to China where they are used as medicine. Despite Indian laws,

◀ *These fishing-cats are eight weeks' old and are living up to their name! Almost all members of the cat family have claws that can be pulled back into their paws when they are not needed for hunting. The fishing-cat's claws are permanently extended, enabling it to grip muddy surfaces more easily.*

▶ *The one-horned rhinoceros, still listed as an endangered species but now protected in India's national parks. It measures up to 5.7 feet (1.75 meters) tall at the shoulder, and its single horn grows to 12 inches (one-third of a meter) in length.*

poaching and smuggling wild animals continues on a huge scale.

PROTECTION PLAN

In 1972 the Indian government began to plan for the protection of wildlife and the re-planting of forests. Animal species, such as the one-horned rhinoceros that was surviving only in the hills of Assam to the north of Bangladesh, were re-introduced to the new national parks that were set up. The Corbett and Dudwha National Parks on the northern edge of the upper Ganges plain provide refuge for tigers, rhinos, leopards, the tree-climbing sloth bear, deer, and two species of crocodile, the mugger and the gharial. But for one species, protection has come too late. In 1994 the death was announced of India's last cheetah, the fastest animal on Earth.

The forestry program aims to increase the area of India's forests from about 9 per cent in 1985 to 30 per cent by 2012. It has run into problems because people in the farming villages rely on wood for fuel. For

◀ *The Royal Bengal tiger likes to laze in the water, but it is also a strong swimmer, using its powerful paws as paddles and its tail as a rudder.*

many of them the only other choice is paraffin, but this is too expensive. There is also an urgent need for more living space. Farmland is too valuable to be used for housing, so forest land is often cleared. The result is that while new trees are being planted, older ones are being cut down.

SUNDARBANS REFUGE

Bangladesh was also once the home of tigers, leopards, elephants, wild boar and deer. Only 60 years ago, these could be found only a few miles away from the cities. But hunters and the growth of the cities have driven them into the tropical rainforest to the east of the mouths of the Ganges, or into the Sundarbans.

The Sundarbans is the area of the Ganges least affected by human activity. It can be reached only by boat, and then only with great difficulty. It is one of the few habitats of the fishing-cat, the only member of the cat family to have slightly webbed paws. The Sundarbans is also home to about 400 tigers and many crocodiles. Both species can be a threat to unwary human visitors. Each year, between 20 and 30 people are killed by man-eating tigers and a similar number are the victims of crocodiles.

THE POLLUTED GANGES

FOR OVER 1000 YEARS, PEOPLE LIVING BY THE GANGES HAVE USED IT AS THEIR WATER SUPPLY AND THEIR DRAIN.

UNLIKE SOME of the world's other great rivers, pollution of the Ganges by waste water from factories is not a major problem in India. There are some black spots such as Kanpur, where poisonous wastes from the process of tanning leather are released into the river, but the main source of pollution is from everyday human activity. Sewage – human waste – is allowed to flow unchecked into the river. The Hindu custom of throwing the ashes of the dead into the Ganges is another source of pollution, especially if the body has not been burnt thoroughly. Some people cannot afford cremation and simply throw bodies in the water. People and cattle wash in the river as part of Hindu custom. This is also the river that millions rely on for water for drinking and cooking.

THE GANGA ACTION PLAN

In 1985 the Indian government, with aid from overseas, launched the Ganga Action Plan aimed at cleaning up the river. The first target was the 27 cities along the Ganges with populations of over 100,000. Steadily, plants are being built to purify their waste before it goes into the river.

Cleaning up the cities is only half of the Ganga Action Plan. There are thousands of smaller towns and villages along the Ganges, and the government could not afford to provide every one with water purification plants. So the second part of the program is to encourage people to treat the river with more respect and not use it merely as a dump for waste.

Here, the government comes up against feelings about the river that go a long way back into history. For example, it helps to pay

▲ *Industrial waste and general rubbish washed up on the banks of the Ganges at Varanasi. One difficulty about cleaning up the river is that Hindus believe the water is holy and will not harm them.*

BEATING CHOLERA
Bangladesh has found an answer to the problem of diseases such as cholera and typhoid caused by polluted water. In 1971 a medical team in Dhaka discovered that a simple salt-and-water solution could prevent the loss of water from the body which makes these diseases so dangerous. Today, teams of trained people work in the villages teaching families when to recognize the onset of one of these diseases and use the solution. The result is that today only one person dies from cholera in Bangladesh for every five who died 25 years ago.

for bodies to be cremated in electric "pyres" in the major cities, but it is hard to persuade people to abandon their old customs.

POLLUTION ON THE DELTA

Overcrowded cities and industrial waste contribute to pollution on the Ganges delta. Bangladesh has 13 million people living in shanty towns round its cities, and their domestic waste flows directly into the rivers. Waste also pours from factories into the Ganges and Brahmaputra. Many of these factories make clothes and other goods for export. Bangladesh needs the foreign currency they earn, so the pollution is allowed to continue. It would be far worse if the annual floods did not wash the industrial waste out to sea.

But this leads to another problem. Bangladeshi fishermen say that they are having to sail further out to sea to catch fish. The waters closer to shore are less and less able to support the fish population. The process starts with the poisoning of the microscopic creatures on which many fish feed.

◄ *Waste from the leather tanneries of Kanpur flowing towards the Ganges. The tanning process uses poisonous chemicals that contain metals such as chrome and aluminium. These metals are released into the river water.*

▶ *Work in progress on an industrial-waste processing plant at Kanpur, part of the Ganga Action Plan. Kanpur, with its leather and textile factories, was identified as one of the Ganges' industrial pollution black spots.*

GANGA ACTION PLAN
INDO-DUTCH PROJECT
UP JAL NIGAM

INDUSTRIAL WASTE WATER CONVEYACE SYSTEM
PUMPING STATION-4 GENRAL MANAGER
GANGA POLLUTION CONTROL UNIT
KANPUR

THE FUTURE

FOR HUNDREDS OF YEARS, PEOPLE LIVING ALONG THE
GANGES HAVE BEEN AMONG THE POOREST IN THE
WORLD. MILLIONS ARE STILL POOR. BUT GREAT
CHANGES ARE TAKING PLACE.

◄ Workers in a factory in Bangladesh making clothes from tied-and-dyed materials. They are working by hand, but many Bangladeshi garment factories have invested in sewing-machines to speed up production.

▶ A change in government policy in the 1990s has led to international companies being encouraged to set up factories in India. This television assembly line is at a factory in Calcutta owned by the giant Dutch electronics company Philips.

FIFTY YEARS AGO, India's farmers could not keep up with the demand for food from the rapidly growing population. The population is still growing, and is expected to reach 1000 million by the year 2000. But the Green Revolution has improved farming so much that India can now export grain, particularly rice, and can produce enough for its own needs.

GROWING INDUSTRY

Meanwhile, India's once old-fashioned and inefficient industry has grown to make India the world's tenth largest industrial country. Indian universities have produced large numbers of people educated in science and technology whose skills attract investors from

◀ *The German electronics company Siemens is another international investor in Indian industry. Here, an operator in Calcutta is making circuit-boards that carry the components of electronic equipment.*

overseas. For example, the giant American computer company Hewlett-Packard has a large investment, owned jointly with an Indian company, in computer manufacture in New Delhi. India has also become a world leader in the development of computer software, with over 700 companies involved. In 1996 software exports earned India $2.5 million.

The development of industry has brought prosperity to many of India's city dwellers, but it has also brought problems such as road chaos and pollution from traffic exhausts. In 1997 the Indian government set up 218 pollution control stations in Delhi where owners of nearly 3 million cars and scooters could have their exhausts checked. The government announced that owners would not be allowed to buy petrol unless they had a sticker from one of these stations.

PROGRESS IN BANGLADESH

The Green Revolution has also improved the lives of most Bangladeshis, but as in India the big change has been in industry. Bangladesh, with its surplus of people who will work hard for low pay, has become an important supplier of clothes to the rest of the world. Cotton has taken over from jute as Bangladesh's main textile product. Bangladesh is the largest supplier of T-shirts to Europe, and the tenth largest exporter of clothes to the USA. The textile industry has been equipped with modern machinery from South Korea, China and Japan. In turn, the manufacture of such things as buttons and zips provides many small local companies with work.

SHADOW OVER THE GANGES

But there is a shadow over the Ganges caused by the competing demands of India and Bangladesh for water. When India built the Farraka Dam, just inside its border with Bangladesh, in the 1970s, Bangladesh accused its neighbour of 'stealing' Ganges water. Now India has a plan for a 350-kilometre canal to transfer water from the Brahmaputra in Assam, to the north of Bangladesh, to the Ganges. This is not an immediate threat, because India could not at present afford such a huge engineering task. But it raises a question for the future.

GLOSSARY

asparagus a plant grown for its green shoots, which are cooked and eaten

carp large greenish-brown freshwater fish with red on the fins

chador a large shawl or veil worn by some Muslim women which covers them from head to foot

chars islands made of silt on the Ganges delta

cholera a disease of the digestive system, caused by drinking infected water

cremate to burn a dead body to ashes

cyclone (tropical) a violent storm, often with heavy rain, caused by strong winds

deforestation the destruction of forests caused by cutting down trees without replacing them with new seedlings

delta flat land at the mouth of a river made up of sand and mud

false-colour satellite image a photograph taken from space that uses unnatural colours to highlight certain features

fertilizers natural or factory-made chemicals that are plowed in or sprayed on land to make it grow better crops

food processing making food out of raw products; for example, making corn flakes from maize

ghat a set of steps going down to the river that pilgrims use when they bathe

glacier a moving sheet of thick ice

global warming an increase in the temperature on Earth caused by changes in the gases that make up the Earth's atmosphere

gullies narrow, steep-sided valleys

hydro-electric power station a station that generates electricity by the action of water pumped through water-wheels called turbines

irrigation distributing water to fields by cutting channels from a river or lake

mangroves tropical evergreen trees whose roots and branches intertwine to form a thick, tangled mass

meltwater melted ice or snow that flows into streams

molten rock rock that has not yet become solid because it is kept liquid by the heat and pressure inside the Earth's surface

monsoon wind that changes direction with the seasons, bringing dry weather in winter and heavy rain in summer to southern Asia

mosque a place of worship for Muslims

paddy-field a field that is flooded for the planting of rice

pilgrim a person who travels to a holy place to worship there

refugees people who have to leave their homes and travel somewhere else, usually because of war

rickshaw a two-wheeled cart for passengers pulled by a man or boy

sanctuaries (wildlife) safe places for plants and animals where they will not be disturbed

sandalwood a tropical evergreen tree whose oil is used as a perfume

sediment ground-down pieces of rock and other material carried along by a river and later deposited on its banks and bed

shanty town a slum area of houses made of scrap materials such as plastic sheeting and old timber, usually without any facilities

shrines places where people go to worship a holy person or object

silt mud and sand deposited at the mouth of a river

soil erosion the removal of soil by the action of wind or water

subsistence farming producing crops for the use of the farmer and his family

tanning the process of making leather from animal hides by treating them with chemicals

terraced (land) hillsides that have been plowed to make a series of stepped, level surfaces for growing crops

textile any material, thread or cloth, made from natural fibres such as cotton or wool or artificial fibres such as nylon

typhoid a serious disease caused by infected food or water

water purification filtering water and treating it with chemicals to get rid of poisons

yaks ox-like animals with thick coats and large horns, a source of milk, meat and leather, and used as working animals

INDEX

Afghanistan 12, 19
Agra 9, 13, 27, 36
Akbar 13, 15, 26, 36
Alaknanda (river) 9, 18, 20
Allahabad 9, 11, 22, 26, 27
Aryans 12, 14, 21
Asoka 12, 19
Assam 11, 39, 43

Ballia 9, 11
Bangladesh 8, 9, 11, 12, 13,
    15, 16, 17, 30, 32, 33, 34,
    35, 36, 37, 39, 40, 41, 43
Bay of Bengal 8, 9, 11, 30, 32,
    33, 34, 35, 37
Bhagirathi (river) 8, 9, 10, 18,
    19, 20
Bhutan 9, 32
Bihar 12, 22
Brahmaputra (river) 8, 9, 11,
    16, 32, 41, 43
British Empire 12, 13, 16, 19,
    26, 38
Buddhism 14, 15, 19, 29, 36,
    37

Calcutta 9, 17, 30, 31, 32, 37
caste 14, 27, 44
Chapra 9, 11
China 9, 20, 38, 43
Chittagong 9, 32, 33, 37
Christianity 25
cotton 26, 27, 43
Cox's Bazar 9, 37
cremation 28, 29, 40, 41, 44
cyclones 32, 34, 44

Darjeeling 9, 21
deforestation 21, 38, 44
Delhi 9, 12, 27, 37
delta 8, 11, 16, 32, 33, 34, 35,
    37, 44
Deoprayag 9, 18, 20
Dhaka 9, 16, 32, 33
drinking water 31, 34, 40, 44

Faridabad 9, 27
Faridpur 9, 32
farming 8, 9, 10, 11, 12, 14,
    21, 22, 24, 25, 27, 29, 30,
    32, 33, 34, 35, 39, 42, 44

Farraka Dam 9, 43
Fatehpur Sikri 9, 13
fishing 8, 33, 35, 41
floods 12, 14, 23, 29, 32, 34,
    37, 41
food shortages 23, 42
forests 21, 39

Gandak (river) 9, 11, 22
Gangotri glacier 8, 9, 14, 19,
    20, 21, 22
Gangotri village 9, 20
Ghaghara (river) 9, 11, 22
ghats 20, 28, 29, 36
glaciers 8, 9, 10, 11, 14, 19,
    20, 21, 22, 44
Green Revolution 25, 42, 43
Gupta empire 12, 13

Harappa culture 12, 14
Hardwar 8, 9, 19, 20, 22, 23,
    37
health 25, 30, 31, 41
Himalayas 8, 9, 10, 11, 19, 20,
    21, 22, 23, 37
Hinduism 8, 9, 14, 15, 16, 17,
    18, 19, 20, 26, 28, 29, 30,
    36, 40
Hooghly (river) 9, 30, 32
housing 23, 24, 27, 30, 34, 39,
    41, 44
hydro-electricity 23, 44

Indian Ocean 8, 9, 23
industry 26, 27, 28, 29, 30,
    33, 40, 41, 42, 43
irrigation 19, 23, 34, 35, 43,
    44
Islam 12, 13, 14, 15, 16, 17,
    26, 28, 30, 36, 37, 44

Jaipur 9, 19
jute 11, 30, 33, 35, 43

Kamla (river) 9, 22
Kanpur 9, 25, 26, 40, 41
Katihar 9, 11
Khulna 32, 33

mangroves 11, 33, 44
Mauryan Empire 12, 19

Meghna (river) 9, 11, 32
Moghuls 12, 13, 15, 36, 38
monsoon 8, 9, 20, 23, 25, 29,
    34, 44
Muslims see Islam

national parks 9, 37, 39
Narayanganj 32, 33
Nepal 9, 15, 20, 21, 22
New Delhi 26, 27, 42

Padma 8, 16, 32
Pakistan 8, 12, 13, 16, 17, 19,
    25, 30
Patna 9, 11, 12, 19
pilgrims 9, 14, 15, 20, 21, 23,
    26, 28, 29, 36, 44
pollution 27, 40-41, 43
population growth 17, 22, 27,
    30, 33, 42

rainfall 8, 9, 11, 20, 21, 23,
    32, 34
refugees 17, 30, 44
rice 9, 25, 33, 35, 42
rickshaws 14, 30, 31, 44

sediment 8, 11, 23, 32, 44
Shiva 18, 19, 28
Sikhism 15, 16
silk 29
silt 11, 32, 34, 44
soil erosion 10, 21, 44
Son (river) 9, 11
Sundarbans 11, 32, 33, 35,
    37, 39

tourism 21, 28, 36, 37
transport 19, 28, 30, 31, 35,
    37, 39

Upper Ganges Canal 22, 23
Uttar Pradesh 22, 23

Varanasi 9, 15, 18, 28, 29, 36,
    40

wildlife 37, 38-39, 44

Yamuna (river) 9, 11, 13, 22,
    26, 27, 36